BASKETBALL LEGENDS

Kareem Abdul-Jabbar

Charles Barkley

Larry Bird

Wilt Chamberlain

Clyde Drexler

Julius Erving

Patrick Ewing

Anfernee Hardaway

The Head Coaches

Grant Hill

Juwan Howard

Allen Iverson

Magic Johnson

Michael Jordan

Shawn Kemp

Jason Kidd

Reggie Miller

Alonzo Mourning

Hakeem Olajuwon

Shaquille O'Neal

Gary Payton

Scottie Pippen

David Robinson

Dennis Rodman

John Stockton

CHELSEA HOUSE PUBLISHERS

BASKETBALL LEGENDS

JUWAN HOWARD

Ron Sirak

Introduction by
Chuck Daly

CHELSEA HOUSE PUBLISHERS
Philadelphia

Produced by P. M. Gordon Associates, Inc.
Philadelphia, Pennsylvania

Picture research by Susan G. Holtz
Cover illustration by Bradford Brown

First Printing

1 3 5 7 9 8 6 4 2

Library of Congress Cataloging-in-Publication Data

Sirak, Ron.
  Juwan Howard / by Ron Sirak.
      p.   cm. — (Basketball legends)
  Includes bibliographical references and index.
  Summary: Recounts the life and career of the former Washington
Bullets, now Wizards, basketball team forward Juwan Howard.
  ISBN 0-7910-4575-7 (hardcover)
  1. Howard, Juwan, 1973 –   —Juvenile literature. 2. Basketball
players—United States—Biography—Juvenile literature. 3. Howard,
Juwan, 1973 – . [1. Afro-Americans—Biography.] I. Title. II. Series.
GV884.H69S57   1998
796.323'092—dc21
  [B]   97-46645
                                                                    CIP
                                                                     AC

CONTENTS

BECOMING A BASKETBALL LEGEND

Chuck Daly

What does it take to be a basketball superstar? Two of the three things it takes are easy to spot. Any great athlete must have excellent skills and tremendous dedication. The third quality needed is much harder to define, or even put in words. Others call it leadership or desire to win, but I'm not sure that explains it fully. This third quality relates to the athlete's thinking process, a certain mentality and work ethic. One can coach athletic skills, and while few superstars need outside influence to help keep them dedicated, it is possible for a coach to offer some well-timed words in order to keep that athlete fully motivated. But a coach can do no more than appeal to a player's will to win; how much that player is then capable of ensuring victory is up to his own internal workings.

In recent times, we have been fortunate to have seen some of the best to play the game. Larry Bird, Magic Johnson, and Michael Jordan had all three components of superstardom in full measure. They brought their teams to numerous championships, and made the players around them better. (They also made their coaches look smart.)

I myself coached a player who belongs in that class, Isiah Thomas, who helped lead the Detroit Pistons to consecutive NBA crowns. Isiah is not tall—he's just over six feet—but he could do whatever he wanted with the ball. And what he wanted to do most was lead and win.

All the players I mentioned above and those whom this series will chronicle are tremendously gifted athletes, but for the most part, you can't play professional basketball at all unless you have excellent skills. And few players get to stay on their team unless they are willing to dedicate themselves to improving their talents even more, learning about their opponents, and finding a way to join with their teammates and win.

It's that third element that separates the good player from the superstar, the memorable players from the legends of the game. Superstars know when to take over the game. If the situation calls for a defensive stop, the superstars stand up and do it. If the situation calls for a key pass, they make it. And if the situation calls for a big shot, they want the ball. They don't want the ball simply because of their own glory or ego. Instead they know—and their teammates know—that they are the ones who can deliver, regardless of the pressure.

The words "legend" and "superstar" are often tossed around without real meaning. Taking a hard look at some of those who truly can be classified as "legends" can provide insight into the things that brought them to that level. All of them developed their legacy over numerous seasons of play, even if certain games will always stand out in the memories of those who saw them. Those games typically featured amazing feats of all-around play. No matter how great the fans thought the superstars were, these players were capable of surprising the fans, their opponents, and occasionally even themselves. The desire to win took over, and with their dedication and athletic skills already in place, they were capable of the most astonishing achievements.

CHUCK DALY, now the head coach of the Orlando Magic, guided the Detroit Pistons to two straight NBA championships, in 1989 and 1990. He earned a gold medal as coach of the 1992 U.S. Olympic basketball team—the so-called "Dream Team"—and was inducted into the Pro Basketball Hall of Fame in 1994.

THE DREAM
REALIZED

The late autumn chill on that Maryland night made a sharp contrast to the atmosphere inside the USAir Arena in Landover. In the hot, sweaty air of a basketball arena packed with 18,756 screaming, stomping Washington Bullets fans hung the hope that this night—November 20, 1994—would mark a turnaround. The victory-starved fans of the Bullets—a team that hadn't made the playoffs of the National Basketball Association (NBA) for seven seasons—now had reason for optimism.

A huge part of the heavy load of expectation rested on the strong shoulders of the newest NBA player—the 6'9", 250-pound Juwan Howard, a 21-year-old sensation who had skipped his senior year at the University of Michigan to try pro ball. Howard's debut this night against the

Juwan Howard handles the ball on a fast break during his rookie year with the Washington Bullets. Though his debut was delayed by contract difficulties, he quickly lived up to his promise.

Boston Celtics was eagerly anticipated by Bullets fans for more than the usual reasons. In addition to hope, there was controversy—and a companion.

First came the hope. As the fifth player chosen in the 1994 NBA draft of college players, Howard was clearly one of the best young players in the country. At Michigan he had proven to be a smart, hard worker who improved every year. In Howard's three college seasons, Michigan reached the national championship game twice and the regional championship game the third year. He possessed not only physical strength and basketball skills, but also the leadership qualities needed to make a team a winner.

Then there was the controversy. The Bullets had hoped to draft Jason Kidd of the University of California at Berkeley, but the Dallas Mavericks nabbed him first. After the Bullets' general manager, John Nash, publicly expressed his disappointment at having ended up with Howard instead of Kidd, the contract talks between Howard and the team became ugly, at one point reducing Howard to tears.

Finally, on November 18—several weeks after the season started and months after training camp began—Howard signed an 11-year deal worth $36.6 million. At last, Howard had realized his dream to become an NBA player. But the contract negotiations were so bitter that Howard's agent, David Falk, insisted on an escape clause that would allow Howard to leave the team after two years if he achieved certain goals. It was a concession that would prove very costly for the Washington Bullets.

The third reason for the excitement about

Howard's debut was his companion. Chris Webber—the first player taken in the draft the year before Howard came out of college, and one of Howard's teammates at Michigan—had been unhappy playing with the Golden State Warriors. Webber asked to be reunited with Howard, and his team worked out a deal with the Bullets. Just hours after Howard signed his contract, Webber was traded to the team. They would be making their first appearances for Washington on the same night. "When I found out," Howard said, "butterflies went through my stomach and a smile hit my face. It's not just how we complement each other on the basketball court. Our relationship goes back a long way. It's great to have him as my teammate and friend."

In recent years the Washington Bullets had not seen many loud, sold-out crowds at the USAir Arena, and for good reason—they were not a good team. They were able to draft Howard because they had the fifth-worst record in the NBA the previous season. Now, though, Coach Jim Lynam shared the fans' excitement. "This is the best collection of young talent I have ever had," he said. About Howard he added, "Juwan brings to the table a defensive presence, a guy that can rebound the ball and a big player who makes other people better. That's a pretty unique package."

Even when Juwan's shots didn't fall, he worked hard on the rest of his game, including rebounding and defense. His total contributions led Bullets coach Jim Lynam to call him "a pretty unique package."

Late in his rookie year in the NBA, Howard shows no hesitation in driving against Dino Radja of the Celtics—the same player who had blocked his very first professional shot.

With four minutes and 21 seconds left in the first quarter of the game with the Celtics, Juwan Howard entered his first NBA game. Soon after, he took a pass with his back to the basket, made a move on Boston defender Dino Radja, spun around and shot—and watched helplessly as his first NBA attempt was swatted away by an opponent who seemed to know exactly what Howard was going to do. Howard sneaked a disbelieving glance at Radja before racing downcourt on defense.

Howard was shuttled in and out of the game as Lynam tried to ease him into game shape. Juwan shot again and missed. Another shot and another miss. Again he shot and again the ball failed to find the bottom of the basket. Once more the ball left his hand in a graceful arc only to clang against the rim.

Juwan Howard's first five shots resulted in a block and four misses. This was not the way his NBA debut had gone in his daydreams as he lay in bed waiting for sleep in his South Chicago housing project. But Howard had handled much adversity in his life, and he knew that the only thing to do was to keep trying—a little harder.

He also knew that if one part of his game was going poorly, such as his shooting, he couldn't get down on himself and let the other parts of his game suffer. Howard continued to rebound hard, play intense defense, and pass to his teammates when they were open.

Finally, Howard found himself in that sweet spot he had known in so many of his dreams. From the left baseline he started toward the free-throw line and cut across the lane. A perfect pass fell into his hands from—of all people— Chris Webber. Howard let fly a soft hook shot that gently rustled the net as it fell through for his first NBA basket.

Howard ended up with 12 points and a team-high 11 rebounds while playing only 22 minutes. Many people took away favorable impressions of him. "They've got two big-time players in Webber and Howard," Boston coach Chris Ford said. "They're going to be a team to be reckoned with."

Despite his shaky start and the fact that Boston won the game 103–102, Howard had proven that he could play in the NBA. There would be many more great nights to come, as well as some moments of heartache and controversy, as Howard helped the improving Bullets—renamed the Wizards in 1997—grow into a contending team.

For Howard, the NBA was truly a dream realized. There were only two things that could have made his debut in the NBA more satisfying—a victory, and the presence of the one person most responsible for the dream's coming true.

2

THE GUIDING LIGHT IN CHICAGO

The South Side of Chicago is a neighborhood of startling contradictions. Vibrating with the energy of a bustling black community, it is a neighborhood of dreams and the hope for a better life. It is also a neighborhood of crime and drugs, a place where teenagers die from gunshots and overdoses. It is a place where children have children. It is a place where things can go terribly wrong for a child if there is no one around to show the way through the maze of dangers.

Jannie Mae Howard was the daughter of Mississippi sharecroppers. Like many other rural Southern blacks of her generation, she moved to the big city looking for a better way of life. Jannie Mae had been a mother four times by her 19th birthday, so she reacted with understanding when her daughter Helena became pregnant while still in high school.

Helena and the father, Leroy Watson Jr., a

Like these young men, Juwan Howard grew up playing basketball on urban courts in Chicago.

The South Side of Chicago, where Juwan Howard spent his childhood, has a good deal of dilapidated housing and poverty. But it also has strong characters like Juwan's grandmother, Jannie Mae Howard, who help guide young people to a better life.

phone company employee, got married. On February 7, 1973, their son, Juwan Howard, was born. Helena was 17 years old and a junior in high school. Because she and Leroy had nowhere else to go, Jannie Mae let them live with her. When they couldn't afford a crib, Jannie Mae suggested they use a dresser drawer. Eventually, when parenthood became too difficult for Helena and Leroy, Jannie Mae began to take care of Juwan full-time. Helena saw her son often, but Leroy dropped out of the picture.

Jannie Mae set a strict course for Juwan. She demanded that he go to school and do his homework. To develop his work ethic, she had him do some of the shopping for the household. As he got older, he began to iron his own clothes. And when the danger of drugs and gangs crept into Juwan's life, Jannie Mae insisted that he be home by sundown. He promised her that he would study hard, finish high school, then go to college and get a degree—something no one in the family had ever done.

As Juwan grew up, he and Jannie Mae lived in several different low-income housing projects. By the time he neared the end of high school they were in a housing complex on 135th Street. Each day Howard rode the elevated train to Chicago Vocational High School. And each day after school he practiced with the basketball team in an unheated gym. "We didn't even have a locker room," he recalls. "We dressed for home games in a history classroom."

If he strayed the slightest bit from the straight and narrow, Jannie Mae let him hear about it. One day Juwan came home with a tattoo on his left arm that said "DR. J," for his hero, the great NBA player Julius Erving. Jannie Mae told him a tattoo was no way to treat his body.

During the summers Howard played in basketball camps and tournaments, and by his senior year he was attracting national attention. College recruiters from all over the country were interested in him, not just because he was a big man with a soft shot, but because of the great work habits Jannie Mae had instilled. "Juwan takes great pride in his game and always plays very hard," said his high school coach, Richard Cook. Some publications rated Howard as the sixth-best high school player in the country.

But not all the college recruiters understood how important Jannie Mae was in Juwan's life.

According to writer Mitch Albom, one team of recruiters spent an evening in the Howard home and directed all of their talk to Juwan and his coach. Disgusted, Jannie Mae walked out to the porch to smoke a cigarette. When the recruiters were leaving, they asked Jannie Mae if she had any questions. "Why are you asking me now?" she said. "You didn't ask me a thing the whole night."

The recruiters from the University of Michigan made no such mistakes. They showed respect for Jannie Mae as well as Juwan. One assistant coach telephoned Juwan almost every day during his junior year and mailed him at least two notes a week. And when this coach visited Juwan's home for dinner, he asked Jannie Mae for a second helping of her collard greens.

After being pursued by Michigan, Illinois, Arizona, and dozens of other colleges, Juwan made up his mind, and Jannie Mae agreed with him. He decided to tell the world about his choice on November 14, 1990.

The day started as always with Jannie Mae waking up her grandson. As Juwan ironed his clothes, he let his mind race ahead. He thought about becoming a star in college, making it to the NBA, getting rich, and finally being able to repay Jannie Mae for all she had done for him.

During the press conference at his school, he showed no alarm at facing reporters. One of his strengths was the ease with which he spoke to people. "I think Michigan is a great school," he declared, "and I'll be able to contribute to their program."

His high school coach was thrilled, and of course the Michigan coaches were more than thrilled. After the announcement, Howard went to practice and then hung out with some friends. When he reached home shortly after dark, there was a buzz of activity about his building. People both familiar and strange were huddled in conversation. They sneaked glances at him, and suddenly a sense of panic swept over Juwan. He burst through the door and found his mother, Helena, and his Aunt Lois in tears, shaking with sadness.

That afternoon, as Jannie Mae was talking to her daughter about how well Juwan had turned out, she had collapsed and died of a massive heart attack. On the proudest day of Juwan's life, he lost the person most important to him.

He had never felt so alone. Juwan was starting on the greatest, scariest adventure of his life—leaving home and becoming the first person in his family to go to college. And he was beginning the trip without the woman whose strong guiding hand had led him there.

But he was determined to keep his promises to her. He would work hard and he would graduate, as he had promised Jannie Mae.

3

THE FAB FIVE

Steve Fisher is a quiet man from a small town in southern Illinois. When his basketball career was cut short by a knee injury, he went into coaching, first at a high school and then as an assistant at the University of Michigan. There a bolt of luck struck from out of the blue.

Just days before Michigan's team was to play in the 1989 NCAA tournament to decide the national champion, Fisher's boss—head coach Bill Frieder—accepted a job at Arizona State. Frieder planned to coach Michigan through the tournament, but Michigan officials fired him and made Fisher the head coach. Even more stunning was what followed. With no previous head coaching experience on the college level, Fisher led Michigan to six straight tournament wins and the national championship. Fisher was on top of the world.

At the University of Michigan, Howard became the first recruit of Coach Steve Fisher's Fab Five—and the key to recruiting the other four players.

By the next season, though, Fisher was hit with a cold bucket of reality. Once the talented players who had won the national championship moved on, Michigan started to slide back into mediocrity. The 1989–90 team reached the NCAA tournament but was eliminated in an early round. Then, in the fall of 1990, when Juwan Howard was starting his senior year of high school, Fisher and his staff conceived a grand plan. They would recruit an entire starting team in one season, and they would go for the best of the best.

The dream team Fisher was after—his "Fab Five," as they came to be known—were all rated among the top high school players in the country. Chris Webber was ranked number one, Juwan Howard number three, Jalen Rose number six, Jimmy King number nine, and Ray Jackson number 84.

The best high school players tend to know each other from tournaments and all-star teams. Howard, Webber, and Rose had played together on an Amateur Athletic Union team and knew each other well. Fisher felt that if he could get one of them to commit to Michigan early, he would have a chance to lure the others. He began by convincing Juwan Howard to come to Michigan. Then Jimmy King agreed, followed by Ray Jackson. Finally, Chris Webber and Jalen Rose committed to Michigan, giving the Wolverines an extraordinary class of freshmen basketball players. "On paper, it is certainly the best class ever," said analyst Bob Gibbon.

This team would leave a lasting imprint on the college game. The Fab Five turned out to be talented, funny, and hard-working. They were also smart and cocky. And they established their own

The Fab Five: left to right, Ray Jackson, Chris Webber, Juwan Howard, Jalen Rose, and Jimmy King.

style with extra-long, baggy shorts, shaved heads, and black socks.

As the first recruit, Juwan Howard was the key piece in putting the team together. The strong sense of family that Jannie Mae had instilled in him made the idea of playing with his AAU teammates, Webber and Rose, very appealing. "There's a very strong bond between us," Howard said when the Fab Five were introduced to the media. "Our relationship off the court is like brothers. We're together all the time. About the only thing we don't do is date the same girls. At least I don't think we do."

Despite these close ties to his teammates, college proved to be a big change for Howard. He had grown up on the tough, noisy streets of the South Side in Chicago. Suddenly he was plopped into the middle of a huge university surrounded by stately oak trees. It had a calm beauty not familiar to a kid from the inner city. Once, Juwan and a friend from Chicago were walking on campus when they heard the unmistakable pop of a gun. Instinctively they ducked for cover. It turned out to be a starter's pistol from the track team's practice.

And there was another big change. Only about 2,600 of the 36,000 students at Michigan were black. Juwan hadn't been a minority at home, where everyone in his neighborhood was African American. But at Michigan only 8 percent of the students were black. Many of the suburban white students had never known black people. They glanced at the Fab Five with shy looks, both because the players were celebrities and because they were black. That took some getting used to.

There were other adjustments as well. Juwan had always been a good student, but college classwork was hard. To make certain they got it done, the Michigan players had a mandatory four-nights-a-week study table and an academic adviser to remind them about papers and exams. There were also grueling, three-hour practices and road trips with airplanes and hotels. This was all new to Juwan.

On the night of December 2, 1991, the Fab Five era officially began at Cobo Arena in Detroit as Michigan played the University of Detroit–Mercy. It was expected that two of the Fab Five, Webber and Rose, would be in the starting lineup. But there was a surprising third on the court when the game started—Juwan Howard.

In a pattern that would mark his career, it was not a great start for Howard. The first time he got the ball he threw it away. He got the ball again and threw it away again. The third time he got it, Howard walked with the ball. The whistle blew and Howard was on the bench after less than a minute.

With only one player taller than 6'6" on the other team, Howard eventually made an impact. Juwan finished his first college game with 13 points and 9 rebounds. But he also fouled out of the game and turned the ball over to the other team 6 times. Though it was a shaky start, Michigan won the game easily, 100–74.

The Fab Five won their first four games before they played a really tough team, defending national champion Duke. They lost that game in overtime, but managed to earn some respect. "They're the best team we've faced in two years," Duke's Grant Hill said. That was quite a compliment for a bunch of freshmen.

By February Jimmy King and Ray Jackson were ready to join Webber, Howard, and Rose in the starting line-up. On February 9 in South Bend, Indiana, against Notre Dame, all five freshmen started for the first time. As they huddled before the game, Juwan yelled, "Show the world, baby." He did not have a slow start this time, hitting jump shot after jump shot. Michigan won 74–65, and the Fab Five scored every point. Juwan chipped in with 14.

Early in his freshman year, Howard showed his trademark intensity (and his baggy shorts) as he joined Coach Fisher in congratulating Jimmy King.

The Fab Five now had fans all over the world. The baggy shorts and shaved heads gave them an identity. So did their flashy style and their tendency to "talk trash" on the court. Not everyone liked this behavior. Some TV announcers said they were showoffs. After beating rival Michigan State, Juwan angered some fans and reporters when he taunted the crowd by waving his arms and then grabbed his crotch.

Coach Fisher came under increasing criticism. Why did he let these players shave their heads and wear such baggy shorts? Why did he let the trash-talking go on? But Fisher's instinct told him that to get the most out of his players, he had to let them have their own identity. They were city kids, and he would let them be city kids.

Michigan finished the regular season in 1991–92 with 20 wins and 8 losses. Though that was good enough for a spot in the NCAA tournament, no one thought a team that started five freshmen could get very far. You needed experience to win it all, the experts said. But after the Wolverines breezed through their first two games of the tournament, a reporter asked Howard if five freshmen could indeed win it all. Juwan answered, "We're not freshmen on the court."

Two more victories followed, including an overtime win over Big Ten rival Ohio State. Suddenly Michigan was heading to the Final Four in Minneapolis. These five kids had become the hottest sports figures in the nation.

In the semifinals, Michigan played Cincinnati, a fast, cocky team that used a full-court pressing defense. Cincinnati players pressured the man with the ball no matter where he was on the court, even 90 feet from the basket. The key for Michigan in beating the press would be Juwan Howard. The plan was to pass the ball to Howard in the middle of the court and then have him pass back to one of his teammates streaking down the sidelines.

The first time the Wolverines tried that strategy, Nick Van Exel of Cincinnati stole the ball from Howard and raced in for a lay-up. A frustrated Juwan made things worse by fouling him from behind. "My bad, my bad," Howard yelled to his teammates. As the game unfolded, the short, quick Cincinnati team continued to steal passes, but Michigan took advantage of its height by pounding the ball inside to Webber and Howard. Michigan wore Cincinnati down in the second half, and when the buzzer sounded, it was the Fab Five who were going to the NCAA championship game. Their opponent would be the defending champions from Duke.

One difficult part of the national championship game is that there is only one day of rest and preparation after the semifinal game. The semi-

Juwan's ball-handling abilities were vital in beating the Cincinnati press.

final is played on Saturday night and the final on Monday night. And when Juwan Howard woke up Sunday morning, the fluttering he felt in his stomach wasn't excitement or nerves. It was the flu.

While the rest of the Fab Five went to a news conference and practice, Juwan stayed in bed at the hotel, sweating, drinking tea, and going to the bathroom. On Monday morning Juwan was still weak, but well enough to eat. This time the fluttering he felt was nerves. "Man, I don't want to make a dumb play, you know?" Howard said at breakfast. His teammates nodded their heads. They all had the same fear.

That night, the Metrodome in Minneapolis was jammed with 50,379 people who were screaming their heads off a full hour before the game started. The pep bands from the two schools blasted out their fight songs. Squads of cheerleaders were leaping and shouting. It was a loud, sweaty, thrilling atmosphere.

When the game started, Juwan was still under the weather, but he was working hard and playing well. Early in the game he slapped away a shot by Duke's All-America center Chris Laettner and twice pressured Laettner to throw the ball away. Both teams were clearly nervous, even the much more experienced Duke team.

Late in the first half, with the game seesawing back and forth, Webber made a remarkable play. After dribbling at full speed down the right side of the court, he threw a behind-the-back bounce pass—the hardest pass in basketball—to Rob Pelinka for a lay-up. The crowd exploded in a deafening roar. Juwan, sensing that Webber could rise to a kind of superhuman performance, grabbed his teammate, spun him around, and looked him square in the eyes. "Right now!" Juwan yelled. "Right now! We take it right now, boy!" Michigan rode that wave of emotion to a 31–30 halftime lead. This feisty group of five freshmen was only 20 minutes away from being the national champions of college basketball.

Pure emotion and raw talent can win regular-season games. But winning championship games usually takes patience, discipline, and the maturity that comes with experience. Michigan found that out in the second half. The Michigan players started throwing up long shots instead of trying to pass the ball inside for easier shots. Duke, on the other hand, worked the ball patiently inside, causing a frustrated Michigan team to overreach on defense and pick up fouls. Soon Duke pulled away, and when the final buzzer sounded, Duke had won its second straight NCAA championship, 71–51.

Steve Fisher never felt closer to his players than he did after this loss. As they watched the Duke players cut down the nets and receive the championship trophy, there was no trash-talking, just gentle sobs and the discreet wiping away of a tear. "Cry, that's part of it," Fisher told his team. "Feel awful, but be proud of what you've done and be determined you're going to learn from this game."

Juwan finished the game with only 9 points and 3 rebounds while Laettner, his Duke counterpart, had 19 points and 7 rebounds. Nevertheless, it had been a good freshmen year for Howard. He was second on the team in rebounding with an average of 6.2 per game and third in scoring at 11.1 points per game. And there were more good things to come.

4

THE END OF A SHORT ERA

If Juwan Howard thought his first year at Michigan was a big change from the mean streets of Chicago, the summer of 1992 was even stranger. Coach Fisher took the team overseas for nine exhibition games. He thought the trip would reward the players for their great season and help ease the pain of losing the championship game. Everywhere they went—in Italy, France, Switzerland, and Yugoslavia—the players were recognized as "The Fab Five" and chased by autograph seekers. But they didn't enjoy it. They missed their video games, their music, their friends. And all they wanted to eat was McDonald's food. "I wanna go home," Juwan moaned.

Soon enough, they were back home getting ready for the 1992–93 season, and they were determined to make it a championship year. Many people assumed that Chris Webber would

As his college career progressed, Howard continued to develop his all-around game, including his passing skills.

drop out of college after this season and join the NBA. So this second year might well be the last one for the Fab Five.

As in the previous season, the first big game of the year was against Duke in December. It was played at Duke, where the students are known for their loud, imaginative, and at times abusive cheering. When the Fab Five walked out to warm up, the crowd started yelling "Overrated! Overrated!" Then they changed to "Five sophomores, no title. Five sophomores, no title."

This year Michigan had the better talent, but Duke was still the more composed squad, and Duke beat Michigan for the third time in twelve months. But the Fab Five were definitely maturing. In late December, at a tournament in Hawaii, they defeated three nationally ranked teams—Nebraska, North Carolina, and Kansas—in three nights. In the following weeks the Wolverines ran their winning streak to 11 and climbed to second in the basketball rankings before a one-point loss at Indiana.

Juwan, meanwhile, was continuing to mature as a player and as a person. He was scoring more for the Wolverines and taking a greater leadership role on the team. That sophomore year, he raised his scoring average to nearly 15 points a game and his rebounding to 7.4 a game.

Just as impressive was his schoolwork. As a freshman Juwan had entered the School of Kinesiology at Michigan, a relatively easy division of the school mainly for athletes. But by his sophomore year, Juwan had worked hard enough to qualify for the School of Literature, Science and Art—the main school. He had promised Jannie Mae that he would work hard in school, and he was keeping that promise.

Michigan moved through the regular season impressively and put together a 26–4 record going into the NCAA tournament. The first tournament game was an easy 29-point victory over Coastal Carolina. But in the next game it looked like Michigan would take an early exit from the tournament. With one minute and 52 seconds left in the first half against UCLA, the Wolverines trailed by 19 points. Though Michigan cut the lead to 13 at halftime, Coach Fisher was angry. "Juwan," he screamed, "you've got to work to get yourself open." For Howard, who was always proud of how hard he worked, it hurt to be told that he was not trying hard enough. He went out for the second half more determined than ever.

Webber grabbed a rebound and dunked the ball to cut the lead to 11. Then Juwan tossed a neat alley-oop pass to Chris for another dunk. Juwan next spun around and hit a jumper to cut the UCLA lead to 7 points. The rush continued, and with just under eight minutes left in the game Michigan took the lead

Howard claims a rebound against Iowa's Ross Millard (52) and James Winters. In Juwan's sophomore year, Michigan had 26 regular-season wins against only 4 losses.

Howard (right) and Ray Jackson battle under the basket with Julian King of Temple in the NCAA regional final, March 28, 1993. Michigan pulled out a 77–72 win to reach the Final Four for the second straight year.

67–66. The two teams fought into overtime before Michigan won, 86–84.

In the following game the Wolverines overcame George Washington, 72–64. Now only the Temple Owls stood between the Fab Five and their second consecutive trip to the Final Four. The Temple game was hard-fought, and the lead changed hands seven times in the second half. Once again, Fisher had to yell at Juwan and Webber to get them into high gear. "Coach said that Chris and I weren't doing a good job as far as establishing position inside," Juwan explained later. But the Michigan big men took the coach's advice to heart. Juwan scored 7 of his 11 points in the second half as Michigan defeated Temple, 77–72.

The Fab Five were going to the Final Four again! Still, there were many in the basketball community who did not want to give them their due. The baggy shorts, the shaved heads, the black socks, and the trash-talking at times created the appearance that the team was undisciplined and lazy. It was true that the Michigan players would coast at times against weak teams, but they always got up for the big games.

At no time was that more true than in the semifinal game against Kentucky. It was perhaps the

finest game the Fab Five played in their time at
Michigan. And it was one of the best Juwan had
played to that point in his college career.

Kentucky, which had beaten its four opponents in the NCAA tournament by an average
margin of 31 points, came into the game as a 7-
point favorite over Michigan. The big gun for the
Wildcats was All-American Jamal Mashburn,
the 6'8", 240-pound junior forward who was averaging 21 points and nearly 9 rebounds a game.
The Michigan coaching staff disagreed at first
about who should guard Mashburn. Fisher wanted to use Ray Jackson, but assistant coach Jay
Smith argued for Juwan. "Juwan's bigger," Smith
said. He could keep Mashburn on the perime-
ter and force him to take outside shots, Smith
pointed out. Fisher knew that would be asking
a lot of Juwan, who would have to handle the
ball a lot in his role against the Kentucky press.
But Fisher also had a lot of confidence in Howard.
"Jay's right," Fisher declared. "Juwan on Mashburn."

It was a brilliant move. And it silenced those
people who said Michigan couldn't beat the really good teams and couldn't play defense. It also
quieted people who said Fisher wasn't a good
coach, merely a nice guy with a very talented
team.

More than 64,000 people were screaming their
lungs out at the New Orleans Superdome that
Saturday evening in 1993. As the players were
introduced, Juwan walked to the center of the
court with two fists defiantly raised in the air.
When the game began, the Fab Five, insulted by
being such underdogs to Kentucky, came out
smoking. Michigan worked the ball patiently and
pounded it inside, just as Fisher had told them.

Jackson scored. Then Juwan. Then Jalen. Then Juwan again. Then Chris. Michigan did not miss a shot for the first five and a half minutes, and the Wolverines led, 14–7.

Kentucky battled back. The Wildcats' spurt came when Juwan needed a rest. He had been handling the ball on the press *and* guarding Mashburn *and* making good passes on offense *and* scoring. When Eric Riley came in to spell Juwan, Mashburn went crazy, and Kentucky scored 9 straight points. Fisher sent Juwan back in the game, and he stopped the Wildcats' run by hitting a hook shot. At the halftime buzzer, Michigan led, 40–35.

It proved to be another incredibly hard-fought game, and the two teams went into overtime to settle things. After holding Mashburn scoreless for the last 12 minutes of regulation time, Juwan caused Mashburn to foul out of the game with 3:23 remaining in overtime. Michigan pulled off an 81–78 upset, and Juwan waved his fist in joy when the whistle blew. Despite the energy expended in his heroic defensive effort and all the time he spent handling the ball against the press, Howard also scored 17 points. It was his most impressive effort yet in a game against a big-time college team.

"People don't give Fish his credit," Howard said about the quiet coach who had enough confidence in Juwan to let him guard one of the best players in America. "He's been to the Final Four three times in five years. He's been to the championship game three times. Whatever people say," Juwan added, "you can't just roll a ball out on the floor and let five talented players play." It was Juwan's way of saying not only that Fisher was a good coach but that the Fab Five were coachable players.

The Michigan players won more than a game with their victory over Kentucky—they won a lot of respect. Critics who had said they were just a bunch of showboating glory hogs had to admit that they played a very disciplined, intelligent, and patient game.

Next up was North Carolina and a chance for the national championship. On Sunday, only about 12 hours after the victory over Kentucky, Michigan and North Carolina had to meet reporters for a press conference. North Carolina went first. As always, Tar Heels coach Dean Smith brought only the senior members of his team to the press conference and had them dress in jackets and ties. The Carolina players answered their questions with polite "Yes, sirs" and "No, sirs," frequently glancing at Coach Smith to see if they had answered correctly.

When UNC finished, it was time for Michigan. Coach Fisher walked alone into the huge interview room packed with about 350 reporters. He sat at the long table on the stage and said, "The guys are running a little late." A minute passed, then two, and five. Finally, nearly 10 minutes late, the Fab Five and a couple of reserves walked in. No coats and ties for them—they were wearing sweat pants and T-shirts. And no careful, cautious answers. They were themselves.

"Yo, Fish!" Jalen Rose yelled to Coach Fisher. "What up, Fish!" Juwan called out, waving from the back of the room.

The coach looked down at the table and tried not to laugh, but he could not keep a huge smile off his face. Fisher loved these guys. They played hard for him, and he was still letting them keep their own identity.

A reporter asked Chris Webber if his father would shave his head if Michigan won the nation-

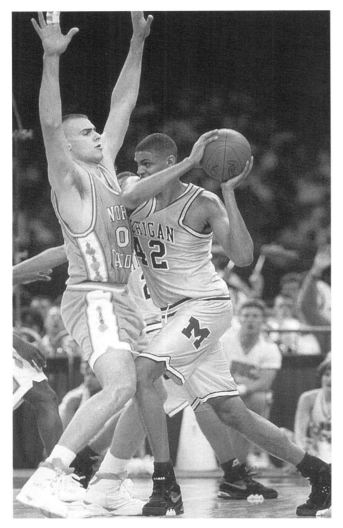

North Carolina center Eric Montross defends against Michigan's Eric Riley. The 1993 championship game became a battle of the big men.

al championship. "Maybe," Webber said. "I think Coach Fisher might go bald, too, if we win."

"He's already bald," Juwan cut in, doubling over with laughter.

That day, the Michigan players who had won over their critics with determined play against Kentucky won even more converts with their funny, honest answers.

The next night, the game quickly turned into a battle of the big men. North Carolina's George Lynch blocked one of Juwan's first shots. Lynch, Eric Montross, and Brian Reese were banging bodies under the basket with Howard, Webber, and Ray Jackson. The Wolverines put together a spurt to take a 23–13 lead, but the Tar Heels fought back to go into the locker room ahead 42–36 at halftime.

In the second half, UNC could not shake the Fab Five. Michigan forged ahead 67–63 with 4:12 to play. Then a couple of rushed shots by Michigan let North Carolina take the lead back, 70–67, as Lynch hit a difficult shot over Juwan. The game came down to one last play. With 20 seconds left on the clock and Michigan trailing 73–71, Webber grabbed a rebound and started up court. Defenders followed him as he dribbled down the right sideline, and when he got to the corner, Webber looked to pass. With the crowd standing and screaming, Michigan's bench yelled at Webber not to call time-out because the team had used up all its time-outs. However, Webber, penned in by defenders, heard that he *should* call time-out, and when he did so, the referees awarded a technical foul. This meant that North Carolina would receive two foul shots and then get the ball back.

The Tar Heels made both foul shots and ended up winning the game, 77–71. The Michigan players were at first stunned with disbelief, then furious. Finally, these proud teenagers dissolved in tears.

"What I want to do," said Coach Fisher, "is put a bear hug on all of them and let them know how proud we are of all of them." He added, "We'll move on. We'll be better people because of it."

The Fab Five did move on. The North Carolina game was the last they played together as a complete unit. Chris Webber left school to become the first player chosen in the NBA draft. But Juwan Howard came back for his junior year— he had promised Jannie Mae he would. And when he returned, Juwan not only took over leadership of the team but also became one of the best players in the country.

5

THE FABULOUS ONE

So much had happened to Juwan in such a short period of time. Could it only have been 30 months ago that he announced his decision to attend Michigan and then came home to find out that his grandmother had died?

If Jannie Mae were with him now, she would be proud, Juwan thought. He had gone to college and made good grades. He had traveled to Europe and played with one of the most popular college basketball teams in history, twice making it to the national championship game. The Fab Five had won 56 games and lost only 14 in two years. They were an incredible 10–2 in the NCAA tournament.

Perhaps most of all, Jannie Mae would have been proud of the fact that Juwan took summer classes in 1993 so he could stay on schedule to graduate from college. Or perhaps Jannie Mae

In the 1993–94 season, with Chris Webber having departed for the NBA, Juwan Howard stepped up to lead the Michigan Wolverines.

would have been proudest of the relationship Juwan developed with Randy Walkowe, a 13-year-old boy who was dying of AIDS. Randy was a big Michigan fan. Juwan visited him whenever he could and constantly brought him gifts. When he couldn't visit, Juwan telephoned. That attention from Juwan helped keep Randy going. And the biggest gift Juwan gave was the loyalty he had learned from Jannie Mae.

As the new basketball season began, with Chris Webber having left for the NBA, Michigan needed someone else to step up and take over as team leader. Jalen Rose might have been the man, but he was too erratic.

Juwan Howard was the man. He was the rock the team could lean on. Howard averaged nearly 21 points a game his junior year—the best on the team—and also led the team in rebounding with 8.9 per game. It was the kind of year Juwan would have loved to talk about with Jannie Mae. In fact, Juwan still did talk with her. "All the time in my mind," he told Johnette Howard of *Sports Illustrated*. And Juwan frequently visited Jannie Mae's grave, especially around Christmas. "See, Christmas is my grandmother's birthday," Juwan

During his junior year, Howard led the Wolverines in rebounding, averaging almost 9 boards a game.

explained. "I always tell her how my season is going."

Juwan was on his way to visit Jannie Mae's grave over Christmas of 1993 when he got an idea. He had a tiny valentine and the words "Jannie Mae" tattooed over his heart. "I wanted to do something really special for her," he said.

Shortly after Christmas, Juwan received more of the bad news he had grown all too accustomed to. Randy Walkowe, his 13-year-old friend with AIDS, had died. At the funeral, with tears in his eyes, Juwan walked up to the open coffin. On Randy's head was the Chicago Bulls hat that Juwan had given him. It made Juwan realize how important seemingly little acts of kindness can be. Juwan helped carry the coffin from the funeral home, and in that short walk—three years after Jannie Mae's funeral—Juwan Howard took the steps from being a teenager playing basketball to being a man working at life.

Howard played the rest of his junior season with greater intensity than he had ever brought to the game before. At no time was he better than in the NCAA tournament, where he averaged 29 points and 13 rebounds. Against Texas in the second round, Juwan had a career-high 34 points and 18 rebounds to lead his team to the "Sweet 16" for the third consecutive year. Then a victory over Maryland put the Wolverines in the regional championship game against Arkansas—just one victory away from a third consecutive Final Four.

The Arkansas Razorbacks had everything going for them. With a 28–3 record, they were the top-ranked team in the nation. The game was being played in Dallas, where the arena was packed with fans from nearby Arkansas. And Arkansas

Howard was a team stalwart on defense as well as offense.

had the nation's number one fan in the house—President Bill Clinton, the former governor of Arkansas.

Michigan fell 14 points behind, then pulled within 2. Juwan did everything he could, scoring 30 points—nearly half his team's total—and grabbing 13 rebounds. Finally, though, Michigan lost, 76–68.

The team finished the year with a 24–8 record. Juwan was voted the regional's outstanding player. "That Juwan Howard, he's awesome," said Arkansas coach Nolan Richardson. "Every time he touched the ball something good happened."

"We have no reason to hold our heads down because we had a great run the first two years," Juwan said. "This year, too, we had an outstanding run when people were counting us out, saying we didn't have any depth or we didn't have Chris Webber."

The loss to Arkansas was a deep disappointment, and now came another difficult time. The experts were saying that if Juwan dropped out of school now, after his junior year, he would be among the top picks in the NBA draft and receive a contract worth millions of dollars. It was an incredible opportunity, but Juwan had promised Jannie Mae that he would finish college. What should he do? He spent many sleepless nights before reaching his decision.

Once again, just as on that fateful day in November 1990, he called reporters together to tell them of his decision. He had decided to leave school to play professional basketball. But what about his promise to finish school? "This university has been here since 1817," Juwan reasoned. "Now it's 1994 and it's still here. So this university ain't going nowhere. I'll be back." In other words, he promised to return to finish the 37 hours of credit he needed for his degree.

Coach Steve Fisher, who had known for a week that Juwan was going to leave school, turned to him at the press conference. "We love you," he said, "and we're going to be with you forever, I promise you." Then, struggling to express what made Juwan so special, Fisher hit the nail on the head. "I've been here since 1982," he said. "We've never had anybody here as good as Juwan. We might have had players with more talent. But he was the best at exemplifying college athletics. We're losing more than just a 6'10" guy. We're losing Juwan Howard."

Howard, as always, tried to deflect the spotlight from himself. "There will never be a freshman class like the Fab Five," Juwan said. "I can't imagine five freshmen starting the final game for the NCAA championship ever again."

6

The Toughest Adjustment Yet

O n a warm summer evening in June 1994, Juwan Howard realized the dream for which he had worked so hard and so long. John Nash, the general manager of the Washington Bullets, stepped to the microphone behind a podium at the NBA draft meeting, leaned forward, and said, "With the fifth pick in the draft, the Washington Bullets select University of Michigan center Juwan Howard!"

Howard could not have been happier. He liked the idea of living in Washington, a city that reminded him of Chicago in many ways, and he thought the Bullets were a team he could play for right away. They hadn't made the playoffs since 1988. But most of all he was just thrilled to be in the NBA—and to be taken with such a high draft pick.

Five weeks into his rookie NBA season, Howard works for position against Anthony Avent of the Orlando Magic.

The joy drained out of Juwan almost immediately. First, word got around that Nash, the Bullets' general manager, had really wanted to select Jason Kidd, who was taken with the second pick by Dallas. Then the Bullets offered Howard a contract he felt was insulting.

Players drafted in the first round by the NBA usually receive contracts that reflect their rank in the draft. That is, the number one choice gets more per year than number two, number two gets more than number three, and so on. But according to David Falk, the agent who negotiated Juwan's contract, Washington's best offer early in the negotiations averaged $2.97 million a year for three years. Sharone Wright, drafted right behind Juwan by Philadelphia, would be earning $3.2 million a year.

Howard rejected the proposal. Negotiations dragged on but Washington was still offering Juwan less than the number six pick was getting. Juwan missed rookie camp, and Nash was furious. Then Howard missed regular training camp, and he was still not in uniform when the season started.

Bullets owner Abe Pollin invited Howard and Falk to come to his house to talk. At that point, though, the offer hadn't improved much. Howard felt the Bullets doubted his ability, didn't appreciate how hard he had worked at Michigan, and overlooked how much he had improved each year. At one point in the talks with Pollin, Howard and Falk went off by themselves to discuss the situation. "That's when I broke out in tears," Howard later confessed.

Finally the Bullets offered Juwan an 11-year deal worth $36 million. It paid Juwan about what the number six pick was getting, but it also tied him up for a long time. "I remember John Nash telling me, 'Here's $36 million,' and he was like, 'Take it or leave it, that's a lot of money,'" Howard said. "And I said, 'Sure enough, it is. But it's not about how much money. It's about what's fair. It's about getting the respect you truly deserve.'"

Howard and Falk decided to take the contract, but with one condition. They demanded, and the team granted, an escape clause for Juwan after two years. He was so bitter about the way the team had conducted the contract talks that he wanted to be able to leave if he wasn't happy.

Later in the year, Juwan and Jason Kidd were on the court talking before a game between Washington and Dallas. Nash came walking over and said, "Juwan, this is the guy we really wanted, but we chose you." Juwan filed this remark away with all of the other things the Bullets had done that hurt him. "I felt really disturbed by that," he said about Nash's comment.

Later, Nash realized what a mistake he had made. "I was wrong," Nash says now. "And I approached Juwan halfway through practice one

Although he started the season late, Juwan averaged 17 points a game in his first year as a professional.

day [during his rookie year] and I told him that I didn't think he'd turn out to be as good as he turned out to be." It wasn't the greatest apology in the world, but Howard accepted it.

Though Juwan started the season late and with a lot of bitterness, his rookie experiences were like those of any other first-year player in the NBA—a lot of learning, some of it the hard way. There was the night he took forearms to the back from Charles Barkley on three straight trips downcourt. There were nights he got pushed around under the basket by Charles Oakley. He also had to get used to losing for the first time in his life. The Bullets lost 25 of the first 29 games Howard played.

"It's tough, I have to admit," Juwan said, "because I'm used to winning. At Michigan I lost only 21 games [actually 22], and I've passed that here already. I have to stay positive. I can't get down. I have to keep thinking we're going to win."

A series of injuries to Bullets starters Chris Webber, Don

Coach Jim Lynam faced many frustrations as the Bullets struggled with injuries. But Juwan Howard, he said in Juwan's rookie year, was "solid like a rock."

MacLean, and Kevin Duckworth forced Juwan into the starting lineup earlier than Coach Lynam would have liked, but the on-the-job NBA training turned out to be the best thing that could have happened. Halfway through the season, Howard was leading the team in rebounding, and he scored in double figures in 17 straight games. He was picked for the Rookie All-Star game.

"Juwan's been solid like a rock," Lynam said. "Certainly our most solid player over the past month and a half." And the more comfortable he felt with the team, the more he let his leadership skills show. In a game against the New York Knicks, Howard was furious when Knicks forward Charles Oakley knocked Webber to the floor, injuring Webber's previously dislocated left shoulder. The next two times down the court, Howard called for the ball and muscled baskets over Oakley. Juwan then scored 6 points in overtime to win the game.

Later in the season, as the injuries mounted, Coach Lynam found himself with only nine healthy players one night instead of the usual 12. "I know we are a little shorthanded tonight," he began his pregame speech. Juwan cut him off. "Forget shorthanded," Howard snapped, glaring at the other players. He made it clear he was ready to play no matter what.

People were starting to take notice of Howard. "He's one of the best young players I've seen," said Houston coach Rudy Tomjanovich. "He's sensational," said Indiana coach Larry Brown. "Howard's going to be a great, great player."

Overall, Howard averaged 17 points, 8.4 rebounds, and 2.5 assists per game in his rookie year. But adjustment to the NBA meant more than just getting used to the better players and the rougher play. One night, his teammates decided to play a rookie trick on Juwan. As the Bullets prepared to take the floor for warm-ups, the announcer called out, "Here are the Washington Bullets!" The other players took two steps

On April 18, 1994, when he announced that he was leaving Michigan after his junior year, Juwan promised that he would still complete his education. The very next spring, he received his degree.

forward, then stopped, letting Juwan run out all alone.

Instead of being angry, Juwan stood in the center of the court and laughed. "It's like I've said all along," Juwan said later. "They're the teachers and I'm the student. That's how it's supposed to be."

Juwan was the student in another way that rookie year. He hadn't forgotten his promise to Jannie Mae that he would finish school. With the help of his advisers at Michigan, Juwan took independent study courses and correspondence courses during his rookie year with the Bullets. He kept books by the bench at practice, studied on planes, and ate in his hotel room as he wrote out school papers in longhand. "By January, I got used to the traveling and the games, when to get rest and when I could get time with friends," he explained. "Then it began to go like clockwork."

On April 29, 1995—near the end of Juwan's rookie year in the NBA—an amazing thing happened. He received his degree from the University of Michigan.

"I was the first person in my family to get a college degree," Juwan said with pride. "You know, I'm very proud of that."

He also had something else to be proud of. He was the first player ever to leave school early to join the NBA and still get his degree on time. That might have been the greatest accomplishment of Juwan's great rookie year.

7

ACCEPTANCE
AT LAST

In his sophomore pro season, Juwan Howard stepped up his performance to show that he was one of the best players in the league. It was a great leap forward, much like the one during his junior year in college.

During the 1995–96 season, the Bullets were once more decimated by injuries, and Chris Webber was able to play only 15 games. Picking up the slack, Juwan added five points per game to his scoring average, raising it from 17 to 22.1, and he increased his assists per game from 2.5 to 4.4. His rebounding dropped only three-tenths of a point to 8.1, despite the fact that he was playing away from the basket more to take advantage of his passing skills. He was chosen for the mid-season All-Star game and named to the All-NBA Third Team at the end of the season.

In his second pro season, Howard raised his scoring average to more than 22 points per game, and he was selected for the NBA All-Star game.

Juwan Howard has played a big role in encouraging children to read through the Reading Is Fundamental program.

And there was more than Howard's personal production. "Just as important," said Coach Lynam, "night in and night out he doesn't take a backward step from anybody. And that's contagious." In fact, Juwan's hard work was rubbing off on the other players. The Bullets, who had been 21–61 in Howard's rookie year, finished 39–43 in 1995–96 and just missed the play-offs.

During that second NBA year, Juwan worked hard at other things besides basketball. He worked with the community in the Reading Is Fundamental (RIF) program, which encourages children to read. "Juwan told me reading is fun," said Lavada Dale, a nine-year-old from Jersey City, New Jersey. Howard also set up the Juwan Howard Foundation, which gave away more than 1,000 winter coats to needy kids in Chicago and Washington, D.C. Juwan encouraged people to donate by offering a free Bullets game ticket to anyone who gave a coat. And he created three Juwan Howard Learning Centers where students could go after school for help with their schoolwork.

Juwan was enjoying everything about being with the Washington Bullets. He enjoyed giving his time in the community to help kids who came from the same kind of background that he came from. And he rose to the challenge of becoming one of the best players in the NBA. But there was still something that bothered him.

In the back of his mind, Juwan was still haunted by the way the Bullets had treated him after they drafted him. He didn't understand why they would pick him so high in the draft and then offer him less money than players chosen later. Deep down, he felt that the Bullets still did not appreciate his ability and his continual efforts to improve his play.

For that reason, at the end of his second year, Howard decided to exercise his option to declare himself a free agent. After doing so, he waited for the Bullets to come up with an offer that would make him feel wanted. He waited and waited. No offer came.

In the meantime, the Miami Heat made him an offer. Pat Riley, the coach who had taken the Los Angeles Lakers (led by Magic Johnson and Kareem Abdul-Jabbar) to five championships and had come within inches of winning another championship with an overachieving New York Knicks team, had just joined the struggling Miami Heat. Riley purged the team of some overpaid, underproducing players and looked to bring in new talent that he could mold into a championship team. The first person he brought to Miami was center Alonzo Mourning, previously of the Charlotte Hornets. The player he coveted most after that was Juwan Howard.

The Miami Heat offered Howard the stunning sum of $100.8 million over seven years. The amount was stunning not just because of the raw numbers, but because at that time no other athlete was guaranteed payment of $100 million. Many entire basketball franchises were not considered to be worth that much. In July 1996, then, Howard signed a contract with Miami.

It didn't take long for there to be a second $100-million man. Three days later, Alonzo Mourning signed a seven-year deal worth $112 million. The one-two punch of Mourning and Howard would immediately make the Heat dominant in their division—the same division as the Bullets—even if it also gave the management the greatest payroll difficulties in the league.

The Bullets were stunned by the amount Miami paid Juwan. They were also embarrassed that they had let one of the best young players in the league get away. The team that had been struggling for respect had made a grievous and very public error.

But all was not lost for the Bullets. Two weeks later, the NBA ruled that Miami had violated the salary cap—the rules limiting the total amount a team can pay for its overall roster. The Heat, according to league officials, had already agreed to the deal with Mourning at the time that Howard signed his contract. That meant Howard's contract was invalid. Pat Riley was furious, but there was nothing he could do. Juwan was once again a free agent.

This time the Bullets responded as if they knew Howard's true value. They offered him a seven-year deal worth $105 million. He accepted. "We didn't get it done the first time. I didn't get it done," said the Bullets' new general manager, Wes Unseld. "But when the second time came around, I was determined to get a deal done as soon as possible."

Howard could not have been happier to be back with the Bullets, especially now that he felt the team really wanted him and appreciated his contributions. "I'm happy and excited about this," Howard said. "I thank God for putting me in this position again. This is where my heart has always been. It was sad to leave a place like this."

Howard was a little embarrassed by the

amount of money he was making, but at the same time he felt it was payment for a life of hard work. "I didn't set the market," he noted. "I'm just blessed to have the opportunity to have signed for the money that I did. This is a dream of mine, a big goal of mine. No one has given me anything—they have rewarded me."

Juwan Howard had always relied on hard work. It was a value that Jannie Mae had instilled in him in his early days when she taught him to iron his own clothes and when she stared him down if he balked at doing the family shopping. And he had always showed gratitude for all he received in life, especially by going back to the community to help those in need of an education or a warm coat.

For Juwan, one of the best parts of re-signing with the Bullets was that he was back with his friend Chris Webber. "We'll be here for a long, long time," Howard said. "Hopefully we can end our careers here."

There was still one other thing Juwan wanted—the championship that had eluded him at Michigan. "If we don't make the playoffs this year," he said as his third NBA season began, "I'll be very, very depressed." And he added, "I'm not going to be satisfied until I get a ring."

His friendship with teammate Chris Webber was one of the main reasons Howard wanted to stay in Washington.

Wearing the new uniform of the Washington Wizards, Howard pats the head of a young fan after an exhibition game in Tokyo, August 1997.

As it turned out, the 1996–97 season had its ups and downs. After the team lost by more than 20 points in three straight road games, Coach Jim Lynam was fired and replaced by Bernie Bickerstaff. But the team went on to win 16 of its final 21 games. On the last day of the regular season, the Bullets beat Cleveland to earn their first playoff berth in nine years. Though they were ousted from the playoffs in the first round, experts were predicting big things for the team in coming years as the young nucleus of players continued to develop.

Over the course of that season, with Chris Webber healthy at last, Juwan had fewer scoring opportunities than the season before. Still he made a rock-solid contribution, averaging over 19 points a game, 8 rebounds, and nearly 4 assists. He played every one of the team's 82 games, averaging 40.5 minutes a game, fifth in the league.

Before the 1997–98 season began, the team renamed itself the Washington Wizards, seeking to avoid the violent associations of the name Bullets. At the gala ceremony in July 1997 unveiling the new logo and colors, it was Juwan Howard, of all people, who strolled down the runway. The player who had thought himself unwanted was chosen to model the team's sleek new uniform. "I was a little nervous and not sure what to do on the runway," he admitted, "but everyone tells me I'm a natural. But don't worry, I'm not making any career changes. I'm definitely sticking to basketball."

You can bet that Juwan will stick to basketball. And if he finally wins his championship ring, you can also bet that he will travel to that cemetery in Chicago, stand near a humble gravestone, and tell Jannie Mae how his team won the NBA championship, how he contributed to the team, and—most of all—how she made it all possible by taking him in, raising him, and teaching him values.

And he'll leave that lonely spot with the comfort of knowing he kept all of his promises to Jannie Mae. That was all she would have asked.

CHRONOLOGY

1973   Born in Chicago on February 7 to 17-year-old Helena Watson.

1990   On the day he announces he will attend the University of Michigan, the grandmother who raised him, Jannie Mae Howard, dies after a heart attack.

1992   The "Fab Five" of Michigan reach the NCAA championship game, where they lose to Duke, 71–51.

1993   Michigan again reaches the NCAA championship, this time losing to North Carolina, 77–71.

1994   Howard is selected with the fifth pick in the NBA draft by the Washington Bullets.

1995   Howard receives his bachelor's degree from Michigan, becoming the first NBA player to leave school early and still graduate on time.

1996   Howard signs as a free agent with the Miami Heat for over $100 million. Two weeks later, the NBA rules the contract with Miami is illegal. Soon after, Howard signs a new contract with Washington.

FURTHER READING

Albom, Mitch. *Fab Five.* New York: Warner Books, 1993.

Howard, Johnette. "Cleaning Up: Juwan Howard, A Do-Everything Forward the Bullets Resignedly Drafted, Is Wiping Out His NBA Opponents." *Sports Illustrated,* February 26, 1996.

The Official Site of the Washington Wizards. World Wide Web. http://www.nba.com/wizards/.

STATISTICS

JUWAN HOWARD

SEASON	TEAM	G	FG%	FT%	RPG	APG	PPG
1991–92	Michigan	34	.450	.688	6.2	1.8	11.1
1992–93	Michigan	36	.506	.700	7.4	1.9	14.6
1993–94	Michigan	30	.557	.675	8.9	2.4	20.8
TOTALS		100	.510	.688	7.5	2.0	15.3

SEASON	TEAM	G	FG%	3P%	FT%	STL	BLK	RPG	APG	PPG
1994–95	Washington	65	.489	.000	.664	52	15	8.4	2.5	17.0
1995–96	Washington	81	.489	.308	.749	67	39	8.1	4.4	22.1
1996–97	Washington	82	.486	.000	.756	93	23	8.0	3.8	19.1
TOTALS		228	.488	.182	.729	212	77	8.1	3.7	19.6
Playoffs		3	.465	—	.889	2	2	6.0	1.7	18.7

G	games played
FG%	field goal percentage
3P%	three-point goal percentage
FT%	free-throw percentage
STL	steals
BLK	blocks
RPG	rebounds per game
APG	assists per game
PPG	points per game

ABOUT THE AUTHOR

Ron Sirak, a sportswriter for the Associated Press, has covered four NCAA championship games, including the two trips the Michigan Fab Five made to the title game. He is also the author of a biography of golfer Greg Norman published by Chelsea House. He lives in New York City with his wife and three daughters.

INDEX

PICTURE CREDITS
AP/Wide World Photos: pp. 2, 11, 12, 30, 33, 34, 46, 50, 52, 54, 59, 60; Jeff Fishbein/The Sporting News: p. 8; C. C. Towle: pp. 14, 16; The University of Michigan/Athletic Public Relations, Photo by Bob Kalmbach: pp. 20, 23, 25, 40, 42, 44; ©1992/93 Rich Clarkson/NCAA Photos: pp. 27, 38; Clay Shaw/The Sporting News: p. 49; Courtesy Reading Is Fundamental, Washington, DC: p. 56. Photo research by Susan G. Holtz.